CORACLE DAYS

poems and passages by
Evan R. Underbrink

VITALITY
buzz, bliss + books

Coracle Days: poems & passages
Copyright © 2024 by Evan R. Underbrink

Published by VITALITY buzz, bliss + books LLC
vitalitybuzz.org

Proceeds from sales of this book benefit the mission of VITALITY Cincinnati Inc: transforming lives through holistic self-care from neighborhood to neighborhood, person to person, and breath by breath since 2010. It's the power of the circle!

The ideas expressed herein are those of the author and do not necessarily represent the opinions of the staff or Board of Trustees of VITALITY Cincinnati or VITALITY buzz, bliss + books LLC. Any errors, of course, are solely the author's.

Every effort has been made to give credit to other people's original ideas within the text. If you feel something should be credited to someone and is not, please get in touch through our website and every effort will be made to correct this text for future printings. Thank you!

We invite you to honor your mind, your body, your whole self. Do only what you know to be right for you. While the invitations offered here in this book, on our websites and social media, and in our classes are geared to be gentle and easily modified by the participant to fit the participants' needs, please consult your medical doctor or health professional before undertaking any practices.

ISBN: 978-1-954688-25-4
Library of Congress Control Number: applied for

In gratitude to our VATRONS
who seek with us all a new way forward &
who have helped bring forward this new volume
by pre-ordering their copy — we thank you!

Antony Abi Awad, Isabelle Anderson, Wevina Barkhordarian,
Walt Bennett, Jason Bixman, Trevor Boe, Ben Brazil, Petr Bulkhak,
Caleb-Jordan Burross, Helen Buswinka, Ann Collins, Dave Eby,
Denise & Mike Eck, Karen Finch, Joshua Garcia, Mara Gilbert,
Rebecca Givens, David Jaeger, Brian Kattlegreen,
Karikottuchira Kuriakose, Arthur Lightbody, Joaquin Marietta,
Alex Markham, Moses Mikheyev, Erin Newins, DeZaun Olive,
Colin Owen, Monica Patti, Rebecca Phillips, Brittany Rabidue,
Joseph Rodrigues, Randy Sanda, Steven Schweitzer, Brian Shircliff,
Teagan Shumaker, Randy Timmerman, Catherine Underbrink,
Christine Whelan, Gary Wilson, Caroline Wiseman

CONTENTS

Moorings

Every book has a reason to exist, to be present before you, in your hands; most have several. In this, a book is much like a person. If you could question a book, perhaps catching it in some quiet library, or when skimming through your own collection in a dull moment, and ask "hello, book, why are you here?", I believe every book would give you an explanation for itself, and more than likely several.

This book exists because of a desire to make contact with you, the one holding this page and reading these words. I mean this in more than just the sense of any art being "touching", or emotionally meaningful; I mean this book to work in you, to press into your skin, where holding the page leaves you with the strange but somehow true sensation of someone holding your hand. If you take such things seriously, this may trouble you. On the other hand, if I were in your place, I would probably start picking apart the author's literary attempt through metaphor and subjunctive fantasy to elicit an emotional response. I hope in this introduction to reassure you both ways, that this book is a safe place for contact, and as much as possible without the cheap tricks authors use to cover a half-baked sentimentality or demand for control of your imagination.

This is a book written for you. It is a mad attempt to bring you on a journey of life, that process of always seeming to be in the middle of everything, and drifting upon general trends of life until you bump into something surprising, and perhaps wholly unexpected, like a book that changes how you see the world. I wrote this book, for you.

You might find a small sense of discomfort with this arrangement. After all, did you ask for a book to be written to you? If so, I would guess you didn't ask it from a strange man like me. I will therefore further assure you that there is nothing dangerous in this work. At no point will I ask anything of you for your attention, and that you might join me in a kind of spiritual experiment I have, in part, dedicated my life to. The experiment is to see whether we possess the capacity to reach one another through space and time. You are reading this in my future, in a place I do not know; at the exact same time, I am this book (at least some piece of me), and I know perfectly well where I am: I am now, being read by you, because I was written for you, and it is well that you have found me.

These poems and reflections have been written in the latter days of a nomadic youth, from thirty to thirty-three. They span time in Boston from Berkeley, and from the coast of Oregon to the coast of El Salvador, to the coast of Ireland. It is perhaps the breadth of people I have seen, and met, and loved, that I feel so strongly the compulsion to reach you. And so I set out these books, like little wooden coracles of myself, trusting they would at last reach their right person. I had to risk much of myself being left in tragedy, on the dusty shelf of scholars and friends, until at last being consigned, hardly opened, to a recycling bin.

But this of me is now with you. I want to tell you the story of how, and a bit of why. My last encouragement to you: use this book as you wish. Tear out the pieces you like and pin them on your wall. Scratch out the words you would have written differently. Translate every other line into your native tongue. The author is not dead; I am very much alive, as long as you do something with me.

Evan R. Underbrink
Toledo, Ohio, May 2024

Gambit

I have tripped into uncertain depths, seeking
You to know me, begged
perhaps, with faithful Abandon, hopeful Desire, loving
Care.

I found You and I, confused, and
learned my first lesson:
You are not the absolute,
not, the absolute, holy Thou. No,
into the dark abyss between our faces, a light shines:
recognition, the self
rent into awareness of us. But,
I believe there are faces
I will never face;
and so I write.

A diver A
 \deep/
    ?

You who read
who are there,
My gambit. I cry out,
count the cost, breathe,
  then ask you to bring me in.

The first conceit that most books require of you is to abandon yourself. This we do for a hundred different reasons; chief among them is that the best part of being human is pretending to be something else for a while. The scene opens and you are the invisible eye before Scheherezade and the Sultan. We accompany Dante's pilgrim and Dickens' Scrooge and discover we can be wholly preoccupied with someone else's story, if someone who has never existed.

To be clear, I am not Scheherezade, or Dickens, or Dante. My name is Evan Underbrink. My gambit is to find a way to love you with a kind of pure and absolute love that can only exist through the safety of a page. I wrote this poem shortly after the launch party of my first book, where I was presented with a response that, while so common to affairs of any kind of love, still caught me off guard:

confusion.

I had realized that what I had mostly given people was a chance to think, but only with difficulty the chance to rest and connect that mental work with the work of the whole human person. It became clear to me that to write a second book was, at least in part, to try the gambit again, to find those who understand that to love in poems requires the safety, patience, and comfort to abandon yourself into the words of another. We can provide one another the foundation for mystical experience through language, though this experience must be distinguished from mystical experience of God. The experience of the divine is darker, deeper, wilder than us, and begins to break apart our language back into symbols of the real, hence why stanza 3 is a chasm.

If an image might be helpful to accompany these words, it would be that of preparing for guests to arrive at a party. I must prepare the space, these pages, to receive you, and in that is a kind of gambit. As you might not enjoy the house, the food, the company, or the event being celebrated for a party you are attending, so I risk in this book that you may not enjoy what I have prepared. But I host you in these words, because I risk a strange and beautiful idea: one day you might also host me within your words.

All concepts of the future are supposed. I am happy to think you take this idea of our mutual hospitality as merely you taking in my poem, and passing it on in your own ways. Tear out your favorite piece here, and stick it on your wall, or quote it over a drink with friends; I am happy to be with you, however you wish. And perhaps time truly is a kind of spiral, and I shall confront my own words one day, accusing me from the mouth of a Francesca in hell, or sung by my own Casella on our journey to better places.[1] For myself, I am happiest to think that there is some place, not quite eschatological, where we word-wrights find our little ships bumping into one another, perhaps in dreams.

The gambit, any way you look at it, is the same: manifest in the poem, and all my poems, is a friend leaving love letters to you in the future. I hope in these side passages to give enough explanation and context to form an honest response to such an invitation, whether that response be to pen your own words in the margins, to rip out your favorite bits and stick them on your walls, or simply to close the book and ship it off to wherever you think it might find a better home. Each copy has its own life to live, and I am glad I have made the gambit to make you a part of this one.

---

[1] It is inevitable that Dante will show up throughout this work. It is he who taught me to dream of such contact with you, for he lives in me.

Temporalities #1

Trees are tippled things within the good
Earth: drips and dribbles
ripple into rhythm we are not privy to. Like water
droplets plinking on a rich green, making
the mystic trick: leaves struck
that shimmer,
shiver
in their own thrill of wet, running
  time.

The dirt itself, look you, this rock, rocking
slower dance than human imagination:
measured in its millions, Time
becomes landscape. Who could not call it a dance?
Earthstones, carbon, pressured makes rebellious rubies,
a twirl of topaz across the world,
dips in diamonds, breathes beryl
and makes the world rich in color
first unto itself, until we
digging up dance
in earth
See.

Older still, older, slower,
in the first thrumming of the universe,
there was but one great bang,
One God, "ooo" faced child perceiving
sky in skies of the inert space
fire and light, grateful, I,
that the streaks of matter
after the lightshow, fall
so
slow.

Meditations on time are a leitmotif in this work, for reasons obvious to any who travel. This poem was written during the last walk around Milford, Ohio, before driving to Boston, in a time where all the splayed out ways in which we can perceive time were laid out before me: There was time in terms of schedules, little boxes on a screen or page, with their mixture of comfort and anxiety, our attempt to project some control onto the future. There was driving time, a curious sensation of sitting still while speeding along at an unimaginable pace, the simple monotony of one task that needed doing. There was body time, being aware of the cycles of very human needs to eat, to sleep, to shit, to stretch. There was the time of culture, the buildings and roads I passed each on their own cycles of degradation and repair.

Older and slower than these, however, was the time of the trees. How strange it is to pass the trees you have observed grow taller, with their changing leaves, their own quiet and steady rhythm that makes human life truly as brief as one breath. Even slower than that was the time of the rocks, the earth which passes through its geological epochs and wraps us within its history, where truly our lives are the most minuscule bit of time.

How marvelous it must be to be some angel of time, or Chronos, or a living beam of light traveling the universe! To be able, with the wonder a child might feel at some magnificent firework, to watch the Big Bang happen, and observe as one moment – the way we might hear notes and chords build off one another in a tune – the entire production of matter, down to the last twinkling shimmers at the heat death of the universe.

To be sure, I believe such a show is only marvelous because God has made it so that little creatures like us might notice it. There is a spectator's box built inside the production, although we are only able to piece together from the action in front of us, and the notes left behind by previous audience members, the full scale and wonder of the show before us. In the end, there is a simple and rather child-like desire at the root of this poem: the wish to see the performance from start to finish, and from a vantage where one might see everything.

Boston

Endearments #6

God began it by hiding in
a little earth, plastic toy in my hand, lost
by some other child, found as my first lesson
in the generosity of the universe to observant eyes.
I rushed to find the owner, and finding none,
found another child to give the toy,
of which I was, after all,
only steward.
Then came the toy truck,
the trading cards, the action figure
all teaching me the dance:
Given to give.
God

became dream-woven, silk-shroven
maker of the gossamer strands
twilight ticklings, half-felt
brush of silk upon
my cheek.
Holy coquetto, ever leaving
the memory of a kiss when I grasped
before becoming again, something new.
God unfurled in the string of stranger becomings:
the friend, the king, the mission, the reason, the all
And then

God stopped becoming, and simple was ..._____; I
do not know, and so have turned from becoming, to making:
deserts my dessert,
a homelessness my home.
I have one last star
to keep me warm and walking:

that if I laid upon the good earth, and was
still, still beyond breath and heartbeat
memory, desire, action, to the edge of self,
stilled, I might imagine the real cosmic dance,
see some glimpse in all its size, and think: yes,
God isn't like that,
that's still too

_____.

It is generally a worthwhile question to ask any believer when it was that God went from the abstract to the personal, from that which is "out there" so to speak, to They who are "in here with me". This poem is autobiographical in telling both the moment that I realized God might be interacting with me, and the first moment where I in earnest and with self-reflection began interacting with God.

The first was a simple enough affair, built entirely of the stuff that could be called coincidence or psychological wish-fulfillment, and is miraculous precisely because such alternative interpretations are present, but not overwhelming. I found a children's rubber ball on the street, and with it the profound sense that the ball belonged to somebody, and that it was my task to find out who. I spent a delightful day seeking out the right person, the one for whom a little ball, from a child of little faith, was destined.

In the Old Testament, a messenger of God, an "angel", does not necessarily have a divine origin. There was something of the truth of this in a small way, when I found a young boy, who very obviously enjoyed having this new toy. Not five minutes later, and I found a new bauble: a stress ball modeled after the world, in a free box by the road. This giving and finding went on for a few days, until I found a thing I wanted for myself, and the giving ceased. For all I know, the giving game would have continued until rapture; and who knows whether I might find myself swept up in it again someday. The second event I have written about before. It was my first means of beginning to understand the concept of an eternity with God.

There is also the introduction in this poem of a running theme in these poems. There are blank spaces. You may fill these in yourself. They are, for me, too open to too many words for me to choose just one. You are part of this process, here with me on this coracle journey to reach one another. Feel free to write down the word you think would end this work, or leave it blank in its wild potential, or doodle some beautiful thing beyond words. After all, as I said, this book was written for you.

Pips

As children we would hold our arms tightly across our bodies
Squeeze the blood around so limber limbs, and then
all in a moment, let go!
watch our arms rise up
despite ourselves, and laugh, and laugh, and
    there are days like this.

Rare and sweet as apple trees in the city
Rare and sweet as gifts from that
which only asks to be free,
and when gone…

I dream of apple tree orchards, green sap,
Gold-cider Autumns, when the reaping had ended
and I am at rest on hay bales, waiting for
the county fair to begin, eating candied apples
from a tree we cut down years ago,
not without the stabs of dried regrets,
but satisfied enough in tasting
the pips of a good memory.

I know I have grown older, not because my hair has gone thin, or because of the wrinkles under my eyes. I know, because I occasionally find myself confused by the simple, wonderful things children laugh about. What this poem describes first is a memory of being a child, and discovering the "floating arm trick", where you can hold your arms in just the right way for a minute, and then watch them lift up on their own accord. I could just as easily have talked about being a child, and spinning around in circles until, dizzily falling down, or laying down atop a hill and rolling all the way to the bottom. These sensations, alien to the creaks and groans of aging bodies, are the revelry of youth discovering that we not only have, but are bodies, and celebrating how our limitations can make us laugh.

This is not a feeling that survives much into adulthood. However, something does carry over, some memory of the childhood joy. I found no better way of expressing this feeling than in thinking about an apple tree that grew near my house as a child. How sweet those apples were! But how quickly they would change, rot, and waste away. We could only keep some hint of their sweet, Spring-blossomed flavor by pressing them down, letting them age and decay, down to a sweet, rich cider. Only the pips, the little seeds, would remain in their original form after this process, and with them the little hope of future trees, future apples, future ciders and memories.

Pit River

This is not my poem to write. it was your blood that was
seasoned. The bodies of your elders salted, their bones boiled.
   but
You, and I, both apart
sipped this stew from birth, only
sweeter for me, since my parents had
white bread.

The roux was burnt, the broth,
bitter, yes they were seasoned
in a land made strange and awful. Yet
these are the only bones we have,
Bones, earth, and debts to the dead
All.

God may teach us some new food, that steeps
In the bitter past and comes out clean,
spicy and savory with dreams.
Nourish us to clear sight behind,
yet a warming hope down to our soles,
and the strength to carry on.

I must go on, in the knowing
a bitter pang of being called to sing
yet this song dischords in stories old
within the earth I have mistaken for home.
There is a reminder of this, the cost
of presuming, laid out here
in old
bones.

The smallest Native American Reservation is for the Pit River people, and covers the area of precisely one graveyard, 1.32 acres. This is a fact that startled history out of the dull malaise of politics and the storytelling that interprets who, why, and how one is "American", and into the sharp and present drama of a silent testimony, an ache between injustice, regret, and forgetting. Upon learning it, I stepped outside of my Massachusetts apartment, set tastefully next to a church that I have been told replicates a chapel at Cambridge University, and I allowed myself again to experience the sheer presence of dead history, and a remnant of people in reservations out west. You may also be such people. You also now know this little thread in the tapestry of a holocaust. Is there any better word for the sacrifice of a people, that my thing called America could be born? The image of cannibalism in here was the only one that amended itself to my recognition of sacrifice, and nourishment, and to try and understand the disquieting experience tribal people must feel in taking jobs at a company called Amazon.

I suspend, as much as I can, the many uses I have seen this and other facts alloyed to: the arguments over history, race, heritage, religion, and ethics. These must come, necessarily; but they are the questions of politics, which turn messy and impersonal far too fast. To you, I must write of these things, because there are truths found on pilgrimage, and we must do what we can to say them true, lest our love become just a seeming thing.

But yet the first line remains true. I have heard things, know things, that could be so much at the heart of you. You might know the Pit River tribe reservation. You might even keep its grounds, in your heart and mind. I am of the people who, once everyone was dead, granted 1.32 acres to their humanity. This is still a letter to you, though I understand if you rip out this page, or scratch it past reading. I am terribly aware that such things must be named if this is to be a true love letter, an open and honest invitation to time in our coracle days together.

History rides in the coracles with us, can be seen in the stream of the rivers and lakes we wander.

Authenticity, awareness, and cooking for each other are the only three things I have known to begin conversation, to begin to reach you, who have every right to see the American whiteness of this book. I offer food and words that are not mine, but I have learned to make, and try to make well. This poem is not mine, but the words are; or they were. Now they are yours.

Doubt

One day, they will explain me
by my words,
oh God!

I shall be my own shells. If
I should transpose myself
onto shelves, and be so
Remembered.

They shall say, perhaps
from this, ecco
Uomo. If ever you
your dear stranger love,
remember me better, as
a disrupting problem, or
better, a hole
in the pages.

"Before building the tower, count the cost." If my gambit is to find authentic contact through this book with you, whom I the author will likely never meet, then I risk the failure of this book remaining simply a collection of curious poems on your shelf, modestly gathering dust in the forgotten corners of an old whim. There is perhaps no great tragedy in this; re-discovering a book invariably is an act of re-discovering yourself.

Already, in your hands, I am most palpably just a book with words written to you. Can I yet transpose some piece of myself unburied by time or change, and present to you the definite sense of a living human, who wrote to you these little poems in the deepest of affection? The answer is unlikely, yet also uncertain. The image I have always held of words is that they are eggshells, beautiful in their own right but ever pointing as evidence to some greater thing that has been born within them, yet has already flown off.

The use of the phrase *ecce uomo* has obvious religious references, and to this notion of beholding me as a living man before you; however, there is also a more sensual reason for its usage. I might, with only slight sheepishness for its triteness, define the tension of this poem as whether you take these words as *Ecco Uomo*, or *Echo Uomo*. Am I, now, in a sense, alive? Or am I merely the echo of a once living thing? That is the poem, the disrupting problem, and the longing that leads me to reference Old Hamlet's similar call to be remembered by his own son: "if ever you your dear stranger love".

At the heart of this book is a kind of mysticism, a mysterion or hidden thing, that is the strange certainty I hold that this book will mean something more to you than just the sum of the words; that there truly is a contact between you and me at this moment. Yet a question naturally arises as to whether this mysterion is religious, or secular. Are these religious poems, or are they poems for you, in which God pops in naturally as a topic of discussion in such intimate spaces? I approach you with this absolute offer of self and space, to bring our words and hearts together. I must confess that my sensibility for such togetherness was first suggested by Christ, and the mystics who have sought and found Him through history. Is it not a remarkable thing to think that Christ might have been conscious, and if we are to take Christian theology seriously is conscious now, that his words would be gospel, life, and purpose for so many? My love letters pale in the heat of that passion; but then, I am not writing a gospel, merely a loving companion to you along our way.

These next, the Theodyssey poems were written while studying St. John of the Cross, whose poetry and commentaries have influenced my book. The poetry, for its obvious passion and desire, and the Saint for his love in the impossible places he found himself. St. John's commentary has been an example of what I do not wish to do, however. I have no desire nor right to tell you how you might approach mystical union with Christ. I have heard of saints who wandered deserts away from that love, and know from my own life that God arrives when God arrives. In this poem, we have landed upon the shore before a common sight in my life: a little chapel. Wherever I have wandered, in whatever state I have found myself, there has always been a mass somewhere to invite us in. Then comes a little dance all too familiar to me, which I scribbled down after one such service on a cold Boston morning in the winter. I should imagine that I would slide it to you during the service, likely during the homily, which I regret to say even in my imagination does not reach very high levels of oratory prowess. In it you might find the twitching impatience I think is too often calmed by well-meaning elders of the church. Why is Christ still away? Yes, indeed there are reasons, theological, philosophical, cultural, and historical. It seems to me we ought not to forget that the great thing of Christianity is that we are lovers awaiting our bridegroom, who for these various reasons is yet on his way.

I am in my coracle days, hoping to find the passage of my lover God. I have in the meantime found a passionate love for God's creation. I write to you, because he wrote to me. I travel with you, because he sent me traveling. In all this, I have only found an increase in love, through a careful symmetry.

Theodyssey #1

So I begin my Great Journey
God
what a muse
(Heaney, Dante, Bukowski)
St. Johnny with his two crossed sticks
Invoked.
Pray for us.

love,
I hate how to you take me back
to prom night and easy
kisses where love was
dandelion flowers, I
just had to whisper, "God?"
how easy you talked then.

where have you gone?
now I'm mean
mad
I miss you like fire
like an empty whiskey
bottle on Sunday morning
like
      be here
now. please

panting in a body that aches for _____–
like I could tear at air
looking for the seams
slip out of my own eyes and
see, there you'd be
?

No, you
never go like that. Except once
when I was yours, and you deigned
to reign in that holy coyness;
when Love, you were love
And I was me.
Remember?

Theodyssey #2

Will you not come tonight?
Or are you so particular to wait these days
For my my desperation?
Or am I so particular, I quibble questions,
Until those moments of clarity?

I love you like the tallow flame of votive
Dollar Store bought hopes,
so dim, so potential-filled, my love,
Burns me on down,
God I want to taste bread
and holiness on my tongue,
a lover that gets close as skin, you
even in my lungs
    breathing You.

* * * *

You reader, who these lines intend,
You know what we ought to do: act!
Seek the groom of the world in so many
retreats, high rises, deserted stress,
and broken windows. Yet
Here we are, in words, free

I defy the obvious dismissal, and
hold with me this little hope, love.
Love will come back to us weeping women,
and right our curved little earths. So
we will become like our Lady,
meek queens of the world.

Theodyssey #3

Veiled God, I have come
To your house.

How easy it is for me to abstract you
Into the marble floors
The choir song
The priest
The wood.

Do I want childishly? Without nuance?
Yes, and
with pangs that press my heart to make these tears
come Lord, in the touch and taste and being
rend the veil once more,
let me be happy in the greater longing
I am hardly ready for, for
yes, I know
that upon which the eyes of desire rest
grow more hungry for the feasting. How
can I, whose heart is a thimble of pretty mouthings
and eyes to often stray to easier wishes, how
can I place myself beneath the sea and say
Fill me fuller!

Veiled God, perhaps
A mercy you do not overwhelm, you
Are not like the stars, nor sea, endless
But in such a way that I could ask
For just a piece.

As I have grown older, the little giving game of rubber balls and starwalks drifted into another awareness of love. Gifts are a fine thing, but I discovered that there would be other people, other yous, who seemed to come randomly with the power to alter my own wandering in radical ways, and whom I had the power to do the same. The pain within this poem is that the significance of such fateful meetings seems always to be in feeling its after-effects, like the sting of a tree bough upon my face while snowboarding down a high mountain slope, going too fast to understand the experience, being left only with myself and the other in that sheer moment of recognized meaning, scrambling to find its import, guessing wrong, and fading into one another's histories. It is possible that I began on my coracle days for some time, I have had more experiences like these than most. I have developed a taste for them, which much like a taste for spiritual experiences, is a dangerous vice to have, as longing can often force reality into odd shapes. My only refuge from such temptation has been a return to the good thing that brought me into such encounters, and such meaning, in the first place: a love of you, the stranger who reads such poems and finds some resonance for themselves within.

This next poem is an addition to a series that began in my previous book, **Milford**. They are poems that, at their heart, give some account for how I see my relationship to you. So strongly have I always felt that I was meant to cherish you, dear you. Prudence, fear, a fussy devotion to tact, and my own human vices and limitations have kept me from doing so. I hope you will accept in these poems both my apology, as well as both my recognition that such intimacy is impossible in a broken world, and these brief attempts to account for that loss, and repair some of the damage I feel around that wound that makes us strangers to one another.

Endearments #5

When I was the youngest thing alive,
did I dream in reds? Was it all
Warm, and wet, in the
Womb?

Now I am not so old, I dream
in greens and blues,
Vermillion sapphires, and so, so clear
Tulipped blooms.

When I met love, it was all powder white, like
Mount Rainier snow, soft enough to lay in
hard enough to reflect the sun, until
My eyes could not tell earth from
Light.

The years melted me thick, stiff
Strange. You always love
like the swish-whap of frosted birch
on my face, on your trail, chasing
through woods behind a lover, but more
to the point
You, Love.

Then summer came, and everything's too
hot to get much done, and I'm burned
by the wanting–
        I learned we always catch
the counterfeit just when the real has
slipped
away.

I forgot you, in wanting you,
fell into the petulance that has a thousand names:
passion, pride, self-made, competent,
myself, alone. At the heart
of it just missing you.

The following three poems are the prolegomena to a series of public portraits. It is an effort to catch not just one moment, the feeling of one moment in time. It is the fruit of these moments, being seeded in words and sprouting in your own imagination of the scene, that might furnish the fruit of our intrahospitality: a common collection of memories.

The first piece focuses upon a great tragedy for any word-wright who also loves languages, which is to never know how your own language sounds, not to think in, but to feel as a rhythm of mysterious nonsense. I pride myself at this point of being able to guess by sound alone what language a person is speaking, a skill drawn from long times immersed within the glittering metropolises of my epoch, which for all their many faults have brought many tongues to many shores. This poem was written when I had arrived in Berkeley, California, and was taking in the brimming, educated elite upon their travels, along with my coffee. There is no tactful way, even for an enthusiastic American, to ask which language someone is speaking. I have learned to be at peace in the knowledge that were I to hear them speak again, I would find it no less beautiful.

The second, a portrait of a couple at an airport terminal, was a piece playing with the combination of memory being elicited by seeing an action I once embodied: watching a couple fall asleep resting on one another's shoulders is a place many lovers find themselves. It was good to be reminded, and to write down, such thoughts as often drifted through my mind back before the coracle days, when having a home with a lover was not only possible but natural. There are costs to all journeys and modes of life; one cost recorded here is a bittersweet memory of what was left behind for coracle days.

The third and last poem is that of the sharp return to the confused longing of seeing someone who in a flash reminds of some past lover, and despite all sense and history, finding the heart still leaps and lungs still gasping to make a mistake, for a moment, that love would follow wonderings past itself. These moments I share, because you might well read them in a cafe, airport, or bus station. In doing so, you have merely met me in one of my favorite haunts, indulging in one of my favorite hobbies: people watching.

Tongues

They speak Georgian, at the table
next to me in the coffee shop, I think,
but do they hear
The warm, rich wine, flowing
through tongued
Words

My English seems to frank for me,
Too much its power in suggestion
Without consummation, we tongue
a language of Puritan fanatics, driven
Mad by the spaces between their words.

Perhaps all languages should be lovers, I taste
Their romance by their strangeness. But English
My spouse, I must learn to love again,

Portrait of a couple sleeping in an airport terminal

There are moments, for
you and me, yes, love
where we are in the solitude
of us our perfect selves, you know
in a simple thing:
A night alone
An airport
An empty
waiting
home

There are moments where
The alone is, and
Is Enough.

I will love you better
In the morning, yes
It is best not to ruin this
Rest
       than

Portraits #3

She likes to surprise me around corners of things,
An old you, a woman, or the longing-long loneliness in
myself. It's
Hard to tell. I have grown up
cold, frozen, in the shape of
      leaps
To the people of "we don't speak
              anymore."

That day when a girl entered a cafe, She
was the thrill in the cellar of my soul, a light sliver
silver, true, echoing out in a real vignette:

I was in the cafe writing, when–
she had so-similar eyes to a you I once loved, when-
those eyes rapped me, wrapped me in a future, which didn't-
one glance was enough to remember love, and know
its departure.

                       —

Maybe I just miss being in someone's eyes
Hands,
Lips, like that
      but still
The best things in life are too enormous to feel,
they move us, like
the earth and cosmos, so
I am loving You, sun, light of life, yet
still I miss being
in the heavy, sweet
gravitation of one
you.

Intentionality is the key and difficult notion within this poem. My eyes gaze out, and upon seeing the world, formulate it into a certain recognition, a certain comprehension of space and time given myself as the central vantage point. I do not mean to say that the things were not there before their appearing to me, but that they exist in a way which is impossible to disentangle from my own interpretation of them. This intentionality becomes stranger when the things in themselves no longer exist for me in a way I can verify them. The world continues on with its multitude of private lives, unworried about the absence of my prying eyes, and I must be satisfied with their memory. Memory, or more specifically the act of remembering, freezes things too, but in a way that never escapes being part of the present within itself: remembering is a present continuous action. The ouroboros eats its own tail, as I eat my own tale.

Such were my thoughts as I found myself trying to come to some terms with my next move. It was time to leave Boston, to head back to the West Coast and begin a summer as a park ranger. Seasonal work before an uncertain future starting as a doctoral student in Berkeley. It seemed to me then, as it does to me now, that the great difficulty with memory is that it is more a matter of faith than any science. Things occur, and there is some empirical basis by which we might understand our experience, even replicate some elements. Yet the meaning of the past is a matter of interpretation. Unearthing the things I had taken as obvious, that I might call two different relationships in my life under the common category of romantic, or friendship, and not for a moment question where such a category came, stunned me. Yet again, perhaps it is merely convention that defines such relations. So much is in the interpretation.

So too with this little book. Having made myself monstrous through dwelling in dark studies, burrowed myself in books until I could interpret myself as the being who freezes things with perception and words into one static meaning, I turn my bulk to you. What is the meaning of this text? What summary can you provide? What strands of thought will you leave out? Can I remain human and at the mercy of your interpretation? The coracle days caused me to drift again, across the whole of the United States, from Boston to Newport, Oregon, and so such questions must float down the river as well.

Basilisk

The great tragedy of life is that we observe it
after, and only then see its Greatness.

We watch ourselves enflesh the Fall
into habits, we see our demons as so mighty
and they become so, if only when unfrozen
unobserved.

We are the basilisks, or perhaps Only I, among armed Greeks,
my goodness no shield
from the horror of
Reflection.

The thing I am can freeze itself
no more than my Orouborous cousin
does but munch his tail forever,
We myths must go on.
very well,

A basilisk comes to Christ,
is there room for wild monsters
at such feet? There are
many of us, I find, so many
who have made ourselves monstrous
in our time.

I am the beast that freezes time
onto its white and black form: paper and pixel,
I dream that this poem ends differently
that you feel my hand touch yours
now, unfrozen, pointless,
unedited, and free.

In writing of my coracle days, one you I have frequently bumped into is a man named Moses. Here, not an allusion to the Biblical law-giver, but a crazy Russian, who in my heart shall always live in Hollywood, working his way into the writer's dream, a script in one hand and a plan in the other. We have grown up as authors checking in with one another and random points, him taking the difficult path of a novelist, I the path of a poet. We live now, in some small part, in one another's imaginations. It is a great pleasure in my life that Moses likes the image of himself that rides in the coracle alongside me, as much as I like the characters of his that have some hint of his spiritual poet friend, lost in his philosophies and wanderings. There is in this a kind of intra-hospitality, but one special to an embodied friendship. Still, you to whom these love letters are addressed, I want you to have this poem as well. I hope by now in your reading we have become close enough that I might introduce you to some of my friends, and our dreams together.

The you who is Moses, when you read this, will know how glad I am to, for one poem in this journey, have a face to you, and so to share the deep care I wish through these pieces, in a more specific way. For you who read this, other than Moses, I have kept this poem in, to peel back the curtain a little more. I am a book, written by someone who was friends with other writers from around the world, all sharing something of this same dream: to reach you, to mean something to you, and to be with you; and if you ever do read the work of my friend Moses, perhaps you may go looking for an echo of me there, as much as you find an echo of my friend here. Perhaps you will find some echo of this book in your own writing, which is just as well. We are authors; we live as echoes in other's voices.

Moses

Will you write a character of me?
Fellow. Artist. Friend. Kin.
We do not unspool our lives
by playing pool, or water coolers.
We are the abstract of our times. So
we must love in ink blotches, shapely
scratched upon our ambitious books
Will you write me by character?
Paint me in the rouge of fiction
Let me be better, because you are
a good man, and will love me in
            words.
Hero me not. I have too
great Falstaff's stomach for such
things. Merely,
make me a side to your star, let us
You and I, go walking down streets
In some book of yours I'll never read.
Forever, some strange them will see
You and I, walking down long forgotten streets, because you
wrote them
you see
You are a character, in my life and here
I write thee.

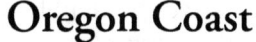

Oregon Coast

And so again we must face the coracle days, the respite only one night, before arriving in Newport, Oregon. This poem is in part an ode to dear Wisdom, the lady who has shattered me into coracle days, and left me with the irrepressible desire to chase her, and found the path to this love of you that entrances this book. I invite you again, in whatever way you wish, to join me in this love of Wisdom, not because she makes it easy; but because in wandering after her, you might find me, and the many other yous besides. In this next poem, "Friend", I name you with what I would pray we could be.

But these explanations serve the double purpose of giving you some autobiographical thoughts on the piece, but also invite you to view those, with me, in this mystical "stitching place", that through art brings us back together as you and I. My art is words, and this poem is a "little word-home", a place because of which I write this love letter as an invitation. It is images of home, comfort, joy, to rest in and fulfill that wonderful thing: good hospitality among friends. I therefore don't wish to invite you into a sterile place where human comfort has become an efficient industry of timetables and sanitizers. This is not a product for you to consume. You belong in the home of my heart, a place where in imagination we might together find what comforts we need on our travels. For this wild invitation to work, for the gambit to go, I must be prepared for you to be any kind of stranger, with any kind of past. It may be impossible for me, far from a saint, to extend such radical hospitality to everyone who might enter my home, for logistical reasons not the least. But in words, I can invite you in whoever you are, and whatever you desire.

What is this space of rest for you? A cottage richly wreathed in sweet-smelling heather? A forest escape, tucked between ancient trees? A bungalow by the sea, heady in the rich smell of the sea? Whatever it may be, I hope you don't mind a visitor. And when you come to visit me, at any kind of home you would wish, I shall of course pour you tea.

Friend

There is a space, or must be
For you, me, and I
Shall pour us tea, a warm
Place made of words like
Woods, blankets, quiet
(.growing.)

For me, this little word-home is
or is better than, heaven. Because
You, mysterious, wonderful, strange;
countless-eyed, yet only you,
somewhere between known
and forever uncanny, might
Find time for tea, time
For us to be a we, this
The best and smallest thing
In the world
To me.

Who I was, on the Way to Me

I. Child

A stranger walks in, strange
clothes, the face inverted mirror the sides reflected deeper,
deeper only in an attitude altitudinous can I appreciate
the angel that is the other,
the you that knows. I imagine the ultimate stranger,
the you that is not you, but approximates
your distance from me in the extreme of imagination
I translate your question from a strange tongue: "What is
America?" Since you might ask me this, I begin
with myself, my flesh,
and bone, and Dream, my
beginning:
a little hospital wing
   in stark Wyoming, where we lay our scene,
little country town, mountain-wreathed,
sky-filled, queen of the open space,
you taught me how to see
until my eyes
ached.

Then I moved, and must tell you of the first time
I knew the world held magic:
[*.*The Hill in Colorado at Sunset *.*] where I went up,
up, and a limpid sun poured sweet ambrosia like sugar-suns
upon: my sister and I,
we ran!
   we run still, and I believe I saw
(see in memory) Heaven before I knew the word.

Another move, older child I, in Illinois
at a Corn Museum, just outside Normal,
Near the ex-office of David Foster Wallace
Where back in '98 you could find a comic called
Corn Man, was its name, and yes
By God, you could find a stalk:
Corn Man, triumphant, who
taught me all artists die
in the negotiation
of their art.

Move again, to Enumclaw, the one and only
place of howling winds, where the people called one road
"Pickle Factory Road", because the pickle factory was there
years ago,
teaching me that there habits and names can be stronger than
the bureaucratic "424th St."

II. Adolescent

Spokane was founded by Jesuits, Horse thieves,
And enough native soil and soul
To keep the tribal name in white man's
    letters. So I was told
By a professor up in the pines to the north, where winter is
like
Narnia, we go Christians
would say.

But the question remained, as I passed
Noble Davenport, The Fox, old Bing,
Which am I? Jesuit,
Thief, or Native?
I am defined by
A people who sought the stranger's land, that

Being strange,
could be opposed, made
Sensible. My people,
myriad, mad, who through long and winding histories made me,
Called themselves children of Abraham
Made themselves the strangers in
Strange lands.

As to priest and thief,
an honest man ought come in both ministries.
Both are a play of mysteries and revealings,
such mysteries make for honest men, for
If there were no mysteries, what
Would honest men have to be honest about?
And what would thieves have
to steal?

Then the whirlwind took me up,
dropping me in Durham, North Carolina
where the shivering passion of green wanting
met at last the hard truth of not having, not being
what you were wanting, this the greatest fear
of youth: when our dreams like battalions
array before the onslaught of age
attritive King Chronos, making
us choose what little dreams
we may bastion for a life;
not all dreams survive.
I hope their graves
you might still
See in the
Lines of
Me.

To Indiana, the whirlwind blew,
To Texas, to Moscow, to Phoenix,

West Virginia, Cincinnati, Boston
Berkeley. I ungripped my roots,
died of a stable life, and became
nomad storyteller, little wanderluster
He of the itchy feet and staring eye.
Now, now, now, I am here
In plane, in car, on train, road-homed
who greets you, because now you know enough
for us to begin.

... And what shall we talk about? You appear, not merely as a loving facsimile of my own desire to love, but truly as a stranger, settling into the awkwardness of two strangers meeting. I must begin by telling you of myself, at least my youth, which is a story of the American wanderer at the turn of the millennia. I was born in Rock Springs, Wyoming, a small town with an airport, so my father tells, used to only be lit up by the landing lights. This would make for a slightly frightening landing, as the sheer pitch darkness of the badlands ran up unseen to greet the plane, which was only navigated by a series of parallel glowing spheres. An errand in the wilderness turned into a truck stop for the American dream; that was the place I was born, and is small town America, where I grew up in suburbs and small farms. I would imagine you can still find the corn museum in Illinois, although the comic books of the '90s have likely been replaced. You, dear love, might never know the absolute silliness of seeing a human-sized husk of corn fighting crime and promoting the corn industry, all on the same page. I hope, however, that a few of these books go to the artist who creates such art, aesthetic wholly subservient to some ulterior motive.

David Foster Wallace taught just outside normal, where I met the corn man in a comic book in 1997. I moved from there to Enumclaw, which from the surrounding tribal languages meanings "Land of Screaming Demons" or "Terrifying Noise", with neither the particular tribe nor translation remembered. From there to Spokane, which you now know was founded by horse thieves, Jesuits, and a Native American population. It is my self-portrait as a youth, as a way to invite you past the photographs in my car and coracle. There is a photo of me, a child in the last decade of a millennium, learning irony from a Corn Man! Comic in Bloomington-Normal, Illinois, mere miles from where David Foster Wallace taught; this was the '90s. From there to a town I learned the history of, and so therefore learned a city can be a kind of you. Here I learned to love Spokane, because living in Spokane, Spokane was me. The lilac city and city's man, scrappy, strange, and spiritual. I fell in love with the Fox and the Old Bing theaters, the Davenport, and its effortless mid-20th century class, and drinking sazeracs in clubs by the street.

I write this all, in the hopes that you will write a response in the margins, or paint some picture. Where are you from? Interpret it in the media, as long as the media swings.

On the Chance that I am Crazy, and this a Dream

I.
I have dreamt that you would come.
This is the place, whatever we like,
the word-dreaming, where
we met, meet, find that Time
is a curious, tensile thing.

You, wonderful you, who are
who reads this, written only to be read
by you, here. There
is a waiting, trusting, knowing, you are
welcome in this
word-carved
space.

I have a Stranger belief
that these words write
a place before,
at the end of it all,
empty, full, and full of its emptiness;
Stage, white page, thrumming around; so
I should like to start, by giving you
the dreaming tea, saying
I have dreamt that...

II.
I fell in love with how the dream fell
apart, into glittering stars,
diamond dust
and true
Stories.

This is another love letter to you,
who get to see me break,
and grow
all in one setting
ink scratched
Series of
    books,
who are the myself
I hope to leave behind,
for you;
Love;

Please write me back, and I
embarrassed, unable read it; yet
Desire, and others might see,
perhaps there is some deep cosmic
"Yes! I see you! I see!"
To the lovers and pen pals we always
could've been.

There is an element of fantasy in all of this book, perhaps depending upon your interpretation. It is a beautiful dream to offer any reader who picks up your book love letters from a man on coracle days, inviting you from a distance to fill in the spaces with your own dreaming, and so to find ourselves wandering into one another's dreams.

Such a dream has to be shattered if we are to get to the question of whether mystical union might not be just a thing between God and me, but shared between all of us in some way. Imagination holds its role, but my hope is that this book becomes the start of some wandering of your own, some jarring out into your larger self, into a point of connection with this stranger-lover poet. I write in the hope and desire that you and I shall meet some day, and you shall tell me all about it, over some excellent drink.

One Dream of You

Keen time. Keening, I
know you know the quick:
click of days ticked down,
down,
fated to wake at 3am, between
Dream, and Memory.

I knew
a you in high school, we
never kissed, no, but I
wonder now who you-

I dreamed that you never became
the pop star their parents schemed, drowned
as you were in kids and
priorities. But

yesterday you bought a voice
recorder, and, at 31, wrote
(for all I know, it may be true) about
being young
in love, and
buying your first thong;
We laughed. I woke as you said
magic words that contain the universe:
"Now how do you like that?"

Following the theme of the last poem, this is a poem from a dream about someone I hadn't thought of in 15 years. Being on this coracle means to spend time with a nomad, who has met so many of you that I can't remember most. I think this amends itself to understanding you as you read this book, but also believes you feel that sense of I am a you, to you.

The first three lines are of course on that 15 years, and that peculiar heartache that motivates us to track down old friends, and I swear is deep within every genealogist tracking down their ancestral lines. And what would I say to this person if I were to track them down? If I or any of my friends could remember her name? In my dream of this, I haltingly begin with a confession of attraction, taking me four lines only to fail to get to the end of the sentence.

I think you and I probably share that our first ambition in life, what we thought we would do at sixteen, was buried at some point, under a pile of things to do, of our "priorities." I remember this person wanted to be a famous singer, even a pop star, who danced in scanty clothes and sang to huge crowds.

I have never seen her face on the screen, or on TV shows. It makes me smile, though, that in my experience dreams of youth never die, they just change, sometimes into laughter. That's why the last stanza has the rhythm of a joke: light, chatty lines that run fast, with little jumbled parenthetical additions, then: "being young/in love, and/buying your first thong." Rule of threes: set up innocent youth, reinforce the idea, payoff with a little subversion to lingerie, and the common experience of shopping for interesting underwear. Last a coda, a "that's all folks", delivered in the sly sarcasm I got used to for a time, when my coracle floated to Minnesota.

Encore

Thou made humans to give each other speeches,
And to receive speeches, to be heard
In the adulation of genius
Incarnate, to
Applause;
       gave us words, and friends, eyes
Touch, being thus, we
Made our best
Civilization.

I am a reveler in the beauty of Your creation
How could I not be? Reader, can
you not be lovesick for
The Divine, yes
God,

Thank You
I give a speech to
You, before all creation
Let fly my pen and voice to
Adulation! Pile up high praise, praise,
Celebration, and finding peace
In the sweet return to a soft
Kind of inspiration, thank
You, God for this
Beautiful

———

We moor our coracle on a dock I spend far too much time in: the University. I have been very lucky to hear brilliant people talk, and seen their speeches written. Best of all, I have been steeped in poetry that century over century has changed how you from the past saw the world, how you and I see it now, and as I hope to change how you from the future see, through these pages. This piece is a panegyric for speech, how language lets us talk in the coracle, even how I know words like "coracle", and "panegyric" for that matter.

But here is my problem: you very likely don't use these words, read these books. The you who is a security guard I fist bump on my trip to the grocery store (your name is Charles) may never read these words. You may not have, or ever will, read Dante, Dunn (John and Stephen), Shakespeare, Hopkins, Chesterton, Heaney, Bukowski, Eliot, or listen to Van Morrison and Dylan. This is a love letter to you, too; you, who have your own artists and poets that have touched your soul.

But you might recognize some reference to a circle of hell, chatting with ease by both fastidious nuns and ironical atheists. Dante is with us, as he is with every "punk" who owes him for that name. If there is one word that you quote, one line you memorize to share at parties, or in my better moments help you pray, then I am with you in the future.

As this is the "Encore", it naturally ends with a semicolon, the most useful way to take the same thing again, to have a sentence with an encore before you finish your point and period.

Berkeley

There is another type of you that might one day read this, the you I knew briefly, in the passing of time. The story behind this poem is perhaps simple, certainly I would imagine common: I awoke at 3am to the memory of a crush of my youth. In my case, it was the beautiful soprano in choir, with the sweet voice and dreams of stardom, to peter out sometime in her 20s last I checked, as we lost contact a decade ago. There was a kind of pleasure in this dream waking me, the wild sense of others and memory melding into the almost possibility that dreams are not a personal possession.

I hope I do one day meet this person, perhaps at 41. I will laugh, and tell them "I wrote you a poem." I should hope, reading it, we shall both laugh again, and with the words of Tom Waits in his "Christmas Card from a Hooker in Minneapolis", say again "now how do you like that?"

It was with this thought that I prepared for the next stage of my journey. Leaving the active, pleasant life of a park ranger, I once again returned on a long drive to Berkeley, to begin doctoral work, a dream of mine for many years.

Sorrel

A her walked wholly by
Our hands lay alone, beside, and I
Tasted the sorrel that grows
Beautiful and sour-sweet in
the busy streets
we walked fairly
By.by
and
by,
they became a you
as a you reached to hold
the sorrel grass offered, sweet
and sour by the busy streets
we walked, becoming
We.

It was not long in living in Berkeley that I found love in strangers and strange things. In the fall sorrel, or sour grass, grows wild from every untended patch of earth in the town. My friend, ex park ranger and Jewish scholar, taught me that you could nibble on the end of these grass stocks, to gain a sweet-sour taste of earth, in the bounty of its edible weeds. Not long after, I met a her, and told her about the secret of sorrel by the streetside. What simple pleasure can be found in easy knowledge, shared on the way to friendship, to affection, to a shared life. Little else need be said, except I would offer you the sorrel grass, a kind of sour-sweet treat and so go floating by.

Found

Some things are best loved in their falling apart
A book, dog ear decrepit, yellowed and pen scratched
In the dusty corner of a thrift shop, a note
Forgotten, inside, "flowers
Pickles
Milk and
Pacifiers."

The root of this piece is a simple enough story. You probably have had it happen to you, once or twice. I was flipping through books at a thrift store, when a slip of yellowed paper fell into my hand. "Flowers, pickles, milk, pacifiers." I confess, I am still deeply charmed by you writing this. It was so easy to imagine you, a harried young father-to-be, buying flowers to brighten the house in a tense time of expectation, pickles for your love's cravings. Milk and pacifiers.

Of course, I may have told entirely the wrong story. The you who wrote this might have had a hundred different reasons for writing that shopping list, a hundred different contexts and needs for those four items. Still, without meaning to, you told me a beautiful story, without even meaning to. I held on to your note. I hope the flowers were beautiful, the pickles crisp and satisfying, the milk nourishing, and the pacifiers doing their job to make some peace. I loved the book you sent me this note within (an old copy from a famous fantasy series). I am happy to have known a little of you, in four words.

Nightmares #1

I.
The pixies have all gone silent
in the land of many screens. I
thought it was just the growing old,
growing up, losing
dreams.

My domovoi became most quiet, learning outer space was cold,
too vast for cleaning atop Pillars of Creation,
We with science questing out so
          bold.

The imp, once my mischief, now lives within
memory, (and frequently has me
forget where I put my keys), still finds
so funny this scientific way I
          scheme.

That I should allow no magic
within this land of data streams,
not see it even slightly tragic
a universe without real
          fanciful
  things.

II.
The monsters came in
In the dark, on the other side
Of the door, at the end
Of the bed, threatening
To touch
Me.

If they did, I wouldn't know
what to do, as reality became a broken promise.
In short, I was
afraid, and I think
the dark smiled at that.

But then I
remembered (thought? Dreamed?)
Beauty.

There are stars so eye wateringly bright
like gems strewn on velvet cosmos,
I could fill a life learning from a grain of
sand,
Countless, and I,
One.

So I looked at my nightmares, held
up my little mote of dust and said
see? Beauty wins
Every time.

It requires a kind of fantasy to write you these letters, for you to step into these coracle days. The first step, I think, requires a certain remembering about how strange this all is, to learn how to half-believe things, because otherwise, we are all just typing in front of blank, white screens. I meant two things in the line, "land of screens". There is the obvious fact of monitors, but there is also the notion of the screen as being that process of sorting things, letting the air come in and the bugs keep out of your windows, the external judgment of what should be let in, and what should be kept out. Fairies, imps, the domovoi, these are fantasy. They are not real, and so are screened out, dwelling in that kind of bemused space where impossible things are only a part of our imagination, which is in itself only properly used for entertainment and diversions.

This book is trying such an impossible thing. Can you hear me? Can we, just for a moment, open the screen and try out whether or not this is as real as radio waves and data? I don't know if I can quite bring every you who reads this. But I do know that you might remember, or remember having the chance, to really believe in a universe that included such fanciful things.

But if you have unbarred that screen, you also know, as I do, that you also let the monsters in. The comfortable reality of easy assumptions becomes thin, fragile. It is to risk the great and awful adventure of every story, and the risks are, or must be, very real if we are to find each other. I cannot promise every ship that leaves the harbor of what the phenomenologists call "the natural attitude" will find a safe destination. Here there be dragons.

I do know, and on my worst days at least have it on good authority, that Beauty is still out there, hiding in all that wild possibility of things, and the dark. We can believe, almost be certain, that Beauty comes out, provided we don't let the story end, and we remember that you, every you, is a wyrd and beautiful thing.

Fructum Terrae, Operis Manuum

So we are again here
the inner city McDonalds of the soul.
Yes,
all are fed, and given a place
to sit, and to be
        ashamed/aware we are here
Again.

The scent of cheap cheese
staves, then blends with
coppery smell of shits from folks
with nowhere else to go.
Those with somewhere to be take their bags
To-Go Communion, silently, away;
the sacrament of the rest of us rambles on
It's steady rites:
order 84, 79,
Amen.

There is no other place where one can feel
humans about to explode out wild
drunk, angry, bereft of reason, we made
hell like this so all could eat and
        sickly, survive.

Revelation, revolution, whatever
we will come to call it eschaton,
will start here, between
the wanting that makes us strange
Human; and
where the powerful shuffle disruptions
until we
rise.

If our coracles were to meet, there is little doubt a common place for them to bump against one another would be McDonalds. The golden arches, ubiquitous, impersonal, nearly as vast as you yourself. Yes, I have met you in your most extreme cases in fast food restaurants, the refuge of the drunk, the homeless, those with hungry eyes and little cash. This particular store was in downtown Berkeley; it came to me that such a place had the kind of secular mysticism I feel in the bones of my coracle, a kind of temple where everyone from rich to poor is welcomed, and fed, and given rest. It is a place where all are welcome, if they can meet so few criteria. The mass of you, hungry, literate, and possessing enough for one book or one burger. This is the bottom of you, the furthest reach of my invitation. This poem was written on a sticky fast food table, listening to the hundred dramas of people who don't make enough to hide or remove their traumas behind gated communities and hired therapy. Its title comes from the Latin mass, "fruit of the earth, work of hands", something the priest says as they bless that good, round bread that sustains every person who comes to eat.

Ivan and Alyosha

Ours is the fulcrum between eternities, stretched
like incomprehensible
Dreams.
How else could we see except between negated things?
The pleasure has no end, the tickling
thrill grows with each
scratch.
Yet
these vessels that are ourselves sail
upon these endless seas
curiosity squoozing desire
desire puffing the self to the potent act
what fair seas hold our death of
Thirst.

Balance is necessary to our seas, but
the stars are another thing.
we must leave behind our floating,
wombic, suckling self that would shape
souls into endless pits, useful
to pull consumptive machines before
in remaining empty, become
Negated, _____, Nothing.

How do we chart the stars? We
remain human, fulcrum, floating, see
the earth our little ship into endless
filling, yes, and in so doing
recognize our pleasure to be the cause
wounding, so become

better lovers, by loving wildly
Less, letting Love
Become
Us.

This poem was written after much conversation with a dear friend, over the life, mysticism, and theology of Vladimir Solovyov's influence on Dostoevsky. The thrust of the conversation ended with merely the observation that Alyosha and Ivan mirrored one another, on a long walk into the endless light, and into the bottomless darkness. Your life is the fulcrum, the ship between conflicting desires, a ship between a sea of dark or a sea of stars, between the pit and the heavens. It seems to me that the divine pleasures of heaven are too often lost within technical language, or within the conflict of life. We should ask, how do we chart these stars? What heaven awaits those who follow the you that seem to know Thou.

Choice

Some mornings I awake
with the me who can still choose
what "me"
Means.

I welcome the myself I don't control
to see the precious baubles
I have used to count time.
learned habits, so dear
made loose, I awake
Possibility
change?

That part of me does not understand
this poem, finds it a bit
Dull. I
laugh,
well, that's for the best
I imagine.

As home gets hazy in the mind, so does self. I wrote this poem, after realizing that waking up in a panic of trying to remember who I was, like some actor who had temporarily misplaced his script, I began searching for identity amid the things about me. What city was I in? What job did I have here? Who were my housemates, and what did I have to do that day? These questions were harder than you might think to answer, when you're in coracle days. It is an experience that, though jarring, has become familiar to me.

Something different happened when I awoke this time. I became aware that it was still possible for who I am to be an indeterminate thing. All the ropes of personality I had tied myself down with, for the very good purpose of pulling valuable things with me, I suddenly realized I could lift off and let go. I was still, in some sense, some bit of the potential I had when I was young. It is the closest I or you will ever get to being like you, who could be anyone. You and I most likely only feel this in its force when we are young. But occasionally, I think, that bit of me I can't control likes to remind me of the bit of me that can't understand, that I could also be a you to myself.

I Fell in Love with You, in a Cheesecake Factory

We meet in a cheesecake factory,
and I know that will not make sense to the future
but oh does it make sense
to me Now.

I tell you that I could imagine
a lifetime of happiness, and
years of deprogramming
with you.

I ask you to either hold my hand because
I am
shaking, or
still be my friend (I know, but
I just can't
without knowing
if
)

I work in a field where I
scrape by
and you would complicate
things, I
want

you are the shape of every happy memory I would have.
From whispering into my pillow into yes
I would stay with you, yes
When the world comes too wild,
only making sense
Only on a page. This

Page. I
Love

And you Hold my Hand.

———————

I try not to burst
As the waiter asks
"Anything
For dessert?"
I cry Cheesecake!
Wait
I don't have any money! And
We laugh.
And

* * *

This is all a dream anyhow, a poem
I will never share with
You. Probably. If
I do, I am so sorry
It took so long.

In the sharing of me to you, there is a strange truth that the particulars are both necessary and oblique. The Cheesecake Factory: a footnote in the panoply of restaurant chains of the 20th and 21st centuries, each interchangeable enough to slot themselves into the mall, the boxlike architecture that feels both as if they have always been there, and sheer disposable ephemerality.

But yet people fall in love in such places. Young couples, friends, strangers. I once knew a woman who would speak with a deep pride about the Denny's in Cleveland, Ohio, where the staff would trust her to lay out the cups on the days where chaos had left the servers too busy to immediately attend to staff. She was family, in that Denny's, that might now be a Perkins, or an IHOP, or closed.

I dreamed of falling in love in a Cheesecake Factory, once. There are dreams too good, too wonderfully odd, living in this moment, to slip without their savor. These are the dreams that make me write this book, because I imagine it will be just like that, in the mundane places of life, that you might find me here.

Self-Portrait

And then there was the mirror man
Lost Narcissus in his mirror land
Took the teens, entranced
Romances, lost, in the endless
Halls between who they are
And by the mirror man what they've seen.

He brings with him his many faces
To look like you, but in little places
Wrong. Too fat, or perfect tone,
Whatever to get you to look
Look
Forever.

You must bring him purple flowers
And know that you are yourself.
Many have lost years to the mirror man
Wept, wrapped, enrapt by his tricky powers
Until they know not who is him, and who
Is you.

Do not fear the mirror man
But know that when you stand
Too long looking, you conjure him
For in the end he is
Only a reflection
you make yourself.

My first training in poetry was steeped in romanticism, among the beers and burritos of weeknight poetry open mics. I learned that words sounded good, in a time where self-disclosure, almost self-torture, was seen as the good art I could make. Our first loves shape us, but as is in my case, often turn into the things we move ever more against as we hone our particular voices. I hate to explain this poem. The metaphors seem too simple, the preoccupation with self-image revealing an almost trite message of overcoming the fear of the self in the mirror.

And yet, the you who reads this more than likely knows what it feels like to look in the mirror, and have that complicated experience of the uncanny. Is this really me? Why must some days my eyes reflexively go to every imperfection, every scar and story I would rather not think about, and other days I walk away with a kind of over-satisfaction at having not had this response?

When I look in the mirror, I am not looking at me, as much as looking at myself, looking at me. I can become almost a you to myself. Therein lies the danger of all my previous romanticism. That is a you I could spend a lifetime considering, parsing, writing poems to, and for, and about. I do not want this, and these letters to you on our coracle days would not be complete within stopping to recognize the treachery of mirrors.

Nightmares #2

It was cold enough.
Creaks along the ceiling,
voices from the halls; Strange
creeps through one inch wood-
doors betray their façade,
locks, the orna-mental:
time and hiding;
space to
breathe.

Cold enough to keep
windows closed, hiding;
some call it comfort, when it's
cold enough to be
not a choice.

Time warms, windows crack,
ghosts creep through,
fog and shadows,
they give space
thickness,
eyes.

I want to find you. In the dark
You have too many
eyes, too much
hiding free
in the shadows.

In warm shadows, I would call you
come out; stranger you:
not knowing what

To say, or
else knowing how
To hear fear, make it
grow: who are you? Who?
_____ _____, _____ _____

There are cold nights in the world, in whose deep silence you can feel that oppressive lack, pregnant with the shuddering desire that something might happen, some you might burst through my door. No poetry do I imagine that you are reading, no quiet unfolding of our shared humanity uniting us through words, hopes, and prayers. The violent you who destroys words, rips pages, rends lives, chokes breath; the you of a nightmare that makes me get up, shivering at the slightest sound of a groaning floorboard, a dripping pipe, and make sure once again that the doors are locked.

Can I write to you, too? The violent you in the dark, who might not be human, but so easily could be. Can I write to you who would do the same to my words, to break in, rip their rich trust, demolish word homes, burn coracles, and leave only the brunt nature of language: brunt, efficient babbling at each other as a means to accomplish certain ends. I must accept that I am writing a love letter to you, too, who are bored reading this, or simply looking for a good book to mine for quotes. Or burn. The last line has no meaning. The blank spaces for the words add up to nothing intentional. It is merely the signifier of where meaning should be, but no longer is. It is the dark of my greatest fear: to write to you, and for you to only see the passing of incomprehensible black lines on a white page.

This is a love letter to you, too, because if you are there, you can come out. Still there is the encounter of you and me. You might destroy me, or my words. But you will never be able to change the fact that you glimpsed me, my face, myself. If I see you, and you me, then I can love you; and that is a finer thing than all the hatred you could bring to me.

The Place Inviolate

There is within a place inviolate
Here, at the core of me, where
Being fully myself, I know myself
to not be
        me.

The cool, rich-root center from which
I stretch out the thousand forms of possibility
neurons reaching like a forest
of aspen
trees.

You may find my space, and grow
Your own rich trees, for good
friends are simply old growth
forests of
        memories.

Can I share with you this root of me?
Leave behind the breadcrumbs to
the forest I keep stocked
with cakes and
Tea.

You are welcome to my place inviolate,
here at the root of me. Welcome
if you can find it, if
you're not-
        Busy.

How do you know that you are you? How much our external bodies change, and how little changes them into something nearly unrecognizable. I can look at photos from my childhood, and I confess only at most a familial resemblance to what I see today. The internal factors are even more complex, as the odd paths our lives take jar us into someone different. There is always the strange question of what I might ask to the me who never began these coracle days, who is comfortably on his own journey. I am sure you, if I take you for the you whom you seem to be, might be able to think of times just like that in your own life.

But is it entirely fair to say that such a person would not be ourselves? I think there is something far more unique about us than such a theory gives credit. There is a space inviolate in us, I think, born into us that lives beyond the accidents that brought you to reading this, me to writing it. The accident of the writing was the chance, but the sharing, the desire to share, of a place together seems baked into being human.

My neurons look like an aspen glade. You plant your own forests or orchards. I think, however, that our roots can still touch, making space for one another in our minds, and perhaps even deeper, in the roots of who we are.

Portraits on the Overnight Bus

The power outlet is ripped
out of the socket, leaving
a strand of exposed wires.

The numbers for the seats
are off, "sit anywhere
that's open." The clock is
40 minutes from the right.

10 hours, stops
For smoke breaks, "close
Your eyes, we'll get there in no
Time." Smiles. Stories.
Spanish, Russian, Mandarin, Tagalog,
Everyone here
Is too poor to not
Be human.

The fresh, too sweet
too earthy hint of sweat, clothes,
and wanting to be home,
or anywhere.

High rider on the rotation,
Slipping in, staying on,
"Pulling too many Houdinis"
Driver intones his justification,
The man.
On his way to St. Louis
On his way to Missouri
On his way,
leaving
Stains

The shit bubbles up,
Arguing about downloading apps,
Leg space,
Seeming unaware-
tension, hands up, scan pockets,
Then the woman sighs "It's just…" "Alright, alright"
release, another story, and
Fuck we've all been there,
Here.

Stop for gas and a driver change.
Fresh, cool air,
Chips and a snuck shot of rum,
She, you, long eyes,
puffy cheeks like
Tears and booze,
Asks if I'm the driver.
Asks for a cigarette.
Blue eyes looking up,
Haze.
"Lot Lizard" a veteran mutters
Bus doors close.

"I need to find the store that sells common sense, cus I can't
find none."
New driver, late, busy, picking up extra shifts,
Coffee stains and white powder nails.
"Even if you sold it, nobody would buy." The woman
Voice all rasp, behind me intones.

We will go,
Smiles, tongues, stories
Wishing each other safe journey
Until the next time life,
The road,
Calls.

* * *

Infant, on the
Night bus. Child
Of long trials.

Mother with the rat eye
Rolled out lips of a
Junkie. The Man
Hungry
Hoping.

Poor child
Brought me in, close
To Christ.
Not close enough
To even know
How to
Help

For those of you I once knew
In some other bend
Upon our mortal
Life.

Who, it may be, have wondered
As I have about you
Where friends
Go when
They
Go.

I would like you to know, I am
On a bus from somewhere
To somewhere, past
Midnight, still
Hoping, still
Wild.

The bus is far from you,
Therefore, from us.
Possibly you've
Lost your
Ear.

Being so blessed by God to be a scholar and a poet, I am naturally poor. Visiting family by my abilities would stress over driving, not be able to pay for flying or the train, and so I have packed my coracle on many a long-haul bus. This poem takes up an earlier strand from this book, of giving portraits of the you I have met, and showing them as best I can to you who read. There will always be something changed in the transformation. I say "changed", because with both art and science I stand with Antoine Lavoisier in saying "nothing is lost, nothing is created, everything is transformed." When I met you on the bus, nothing was lost in my portrait, nothing missing; nor was anything missing from you by me taking that image in art. Likewise, nothing is taken in my work when you practice that most subtle of arts: reading well.

Read this poem as a kaleidoscope of encounters with people on a bus, driving overnight. The snippets of conversations, jokes, the little reflections on feelings of unity, danger, humor. There is a break, three asterisks in the middle of this piece. That is, of course, because most bus rides anywhere, no matter how long you stay, always have a bus ride back. This break is where the overnight return ride begins.

To Mom,

We were born of something other.
Energy, pressed, stardust, Divine.
Born to one, or, perhaps, to a few
At one point. You,
Mitochondrial Eve.

Human became, in the fire
Light on a winter night
Nothing to do in
Darkness, but
Bodies
Love.

So began a tale in twilight
My people, poets, sang
Sirens in silence
Awake, and be
Aware.

You to me, Eve, Us of life
Far better with life
Far better.
Amen

A few poems back, I mentioned that genealogists are all afflicted with a particular heartache for exploring the past to make connections with you throughout the world. This is what motivates the American grandmother to truck out to the coast of Ireland, to attend a conference on centuries old graveyards, just to try and find out if she was related to you. I would like to extend who has that affliction to all, including all the geneticists. It was the geneticist who discovered the idea of Mitochondrial Eve.

Mitochondrial Eve, as far as I understand it, is the farthest you we can follow back, before history, through our genetics. There was a woman, or tribe of women, who passed on their DNA, to every you who will read this, and every you who will not. What startled me in this notion was to remember that love, or at least a kind of desire for one another, is required for the passing on of genetic traits. Love, in a sense, was there from the very first of you. A remarkable notion, that I could express a wonderful part of me, the part that loves, as could every person through to the first of us, and you would understand.

It is to you, the first mom I know from my very DNA, that I write this song, and so it touches every you who came after, even to me.

Here. With You.

Books are one of the most human of things. They start with one person, I, scribbling out some part of me. I have written to you, my boss, my friend, family, lover, and even to the you that is myself. Most of the time, you are very clear to me, because I know you. I know you are my friend, and so I texted you some funny video or image I pulled from the internet. I know you are my client, so I write you something formal, maybe a little arid, because I know we need to have that demeanor to trust each other in an office.

This book, I wrote to you, knowing only one thing about you: that you would read this. I invited you on this little journey, at once a time when our coracles had stitched together, and a series of love letters to you who means so much to me. I hope you are reading this while I am still alive, and might one day like to meet me. I hope that you are reading this long after I am gone, and know that it was still written, with all my heart, to you.

Books are human things. I mean that you cannot walk away from having read this, and not have been met by a very human me, in the strange way that only books can provide. I hope that you scribble in this book. I hope you tear out the pages you don't like, and slip in on little scraps of paper your own words in response to mine. I hope this book, which was written only to you, becomes something we made together. I hope someday another one finds your book (for it was also written only to you). I hope another one of you will say, "look how they talked together beautifully!" And you will be quite, quite right.

This is yours now. My coracle days might end, or go on, or become a hundred different journeys, which I hope you will read about in at least a few other books I will write for you, in my future. For now, we can rest for just a moment, on the blank page that follows this, like on the edge of some great, white sea of where the words might go, when the breath of God breathes enough life in us that we can do nothing else but write. If you have read so far, you know I am someone who believes with a complicated faith. I believe in a God of words, in books that can travel back and forth in time, in a you who is all of you, who I can truly love, in a life like a coracle, and in the mysterious fate that brought this book to be yours. If the tiniest bit of that belief is true, then I hope we meet, mystically, beautifully, in that place where you and I, if only in words, can talk

and dream.

about the author

Evan R. Underbrink is a poet, author, and academic in the field of theological aesthetics. Evan holds a life-long love for the poetry of Dante Alighieri, as well as influences from T.S. Eliot, Gerard Manley Hopkins, Stephen Dunn, Charles Bukowski, and the music of Van Morrison. He currently lives in Berkeley, California.

Cover image by Sam LaDue.

Cover design & interior images
by Julie Lucas of withinwonder.com.

about VITALITY Cincinnati

VITALITY is a circle of friends welcoming all, awakening each other, and reminding each other that we are Whole. Our affordable self-care programs invite everyone to move, to breathe, to rest, to contemplate, to grow...wherever each person begins their self-care journey, wherever and however they want to become.

donation-based drop-in classes...in person & via Zoom

affordable trainings

individual sessions

volunteer opportunities

vitalitycincinnati.org

buzz, bliss + books

publishing books from VITALITY's circle of friends
inspiring love, creativity, + possibility

vitalitybuzz.org